IDEAS FOR USING THESE WORKSHEETS ...

- As CLASSWORK SHEETS, made easier by using them in conjunction with the revision guide.
- As HOMEWORK SHEETS, with differentiated questions to challenge all abilities, similar in style to the National Curriculum Tests.
- As a STRUCTURED REVISION PROGRAMME in the months preceding the National Curriculum Tests.
- As TEST MATERIAL to test understanding of individual or groups of topics.

and last but not least ...

- As an EMERGENCY MEASURE for when staff are absent at short notice.

A NOTE TO TEACHERS AND PARENTS ...

These Worksheets have been designed to give children all the practice they need to be able to confidently tackle the Key Stage Two National Curriculum Tests in Mathematics for levels 3 - 5 inclusive. They have also been designed to be as easy to use as possible. All questions are easy to mark with a comprehensive set of answers in a pull out section at the centre of the book. All the Worksheets are cross-referenced to the best-selling revision guide "THE ESSENTIALS OF MATHS: KEY STAGE TWO" by Hannah Roberts.

A NOTE TO THE PUPIL ...

We hope that you will enjoy working through this book. Spaces have been left for your answers, these are indicated by a ✏ symbol. However make sure you write down all the calculations you make, even if they are done in your head, as you will be expected to do this in the National Curriculum Tests.

Some pages have a 🚫 symbol. This means you should not use a calculator on any of the questions on that page. On any other page you may use a calculator if you wish, but you don't need one.

As you work through the book, have your answers checked regularly and go back through any you have got wrong. If you have a copy of the revision guide: "THE ESSENTIALS OF MATHS: KEY STAGE TWO" by Hannah Roberts, you can use this to help as the pages in each book match each other. Try to get into a routine. Work through the book steadily, don't rush and don't try to do too much at once.

Good Luck!!

**All these worksheets are cross-referenced to the best-selling revision guide
"THE ESSENTIALS OF MATHS: KEY STAGE TWO" by Hannah Roberts.**

THE VALUE OF NUMBERS

NUMBER 1

1. Draw an arrow connecting each number with the value of it's underlined digit. The first one has been done for you.

   1<u>3</u>7 — 3 tens
   20<u>3</u> — 3 hundreds
   <u>3</u>417 — 3 hundreds
   4<u>3</u>29 — 3 tenths
   26.<u>3</u>5 — 3 thousands
   18.1<u>3</u> — 3 hundredths

2. Paul has these four number cards:

   [3] [6] [0] [7]

   He can use them to make the 3-digit number [3][0][7]

   a) What is the largest 2-digit number he can make with these cards?

   b) What is the smallest 3-digit number he can make with these cards?

   c) What is the largest 4-digit number he can make with these cards?

   d) What is the smallest 4-digit number he can make with these cards?

3. a) What is the largest 4-digit number you can make if all the digits are different?

   b) What is the smallest 4-digit number you can make, if you are allowed to put a decimal point in, and if all the digits are different?

4. Bryony has these four different number cards:

   [6] [3] [8] [1]

   a) Use these cards to make a number between 1750 and 2000.

   b) Make a number between 6500 and 7500.

ORDERING NUMBERS

NUMBER 2

1. Arrange these 6 lottery balls in order, starting with the smallest.

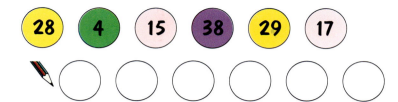

2. In the Globalot lottery, the winning balls were.

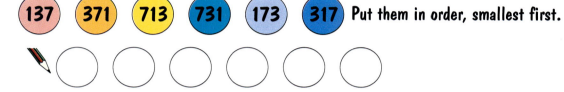 Put them in order, smallest first.

3. There are six different three digit numbers that can be made with these three cards.

   Write them down in order of size from smallest to largest.

4. Write each group of numbers in order of size starting with the smallest.

   a) 2.37   2.29   2.45   2.58

   b) 5.8   5.76   6.0   5.79

   c) 47.23   4.723   4723   472.3

   d) 0.31   0.03   0.1   0.13   0.3

5. Write down six numbers between 2 and 3. Put them in order, starting with the smallest.

MULTIPLYING AND DIVIDING 10 AND 100

NUMBER 3

1. Draw an arrow connecting each calculation with its answer. The first one has been done for you.

   You must not use a calculator.

   350 × 100   3500
   350 ÷ 10   35
   35 × 100   350
   35 × 10
   3500 ÷ 100   35000

2. Put a circle around the number which is 805 × 10.

   850   8050   8500   8005   815

3. Write in the missing numbers.

   a) ☐ × 10 = 6300   b) 15 × 10 = ☐
   c) ☐ ÷ 10 = 82   d) 6030 ÷ ☐ = 603
   e) ☐ × 100 = 2400   f) 18 × ☐ = 1800
   g) ☐ ÷ 100 = 50   h) 36000 ÷ 100 = ☐

4. Write what the four missing digits could be.

   a) ☐☐ ÷ 10 = 6☐   b) ☐1 × 10 = ☐☐
   c) ☐☐ × 10 = 4☐☐   d) ☐☐ × 100 = ☐20

5. Year 6 are holding a sponsored relay race around a 100m track.

   a) What is the total distance covered after 8 laps? ☐ m
   b) What is the total distance covered after 33 laps? ☐ m
   c) How many laps did they complete if they covered a total distance of 5200m? ☐

6. Chocco bars are sold in packs of 10.

   a) How many bars are there in 7 packs? ☐
   b) How many bars are there in 150 packs? ☐
   c) How many packs are needed for 1000 bars? ☐

MULTIPLYING AND DIVIDING BY 10, 100 AND 1000

NUMBER 4

1. Complete these sentences:

   a) When you multiply by 1000, the digits move _____ places to the left.

   b) When you divide by 100, the digits move _____ places to the _____.

   c) When you multiply by 10, the digits move _____ place to the _____.

You must not use a calculator.

2. Put a circle around the number which is 3.5 × 10.

   3.50   3.05   0.35   35   350

3. Put a circle around the number which is 87 × 1000.

   87000   8700   8007   8070   80700

4. Peter has these "operation cards":

   | × 10 | × 100 | × 1000 | ÷ 10 | ÷ 100 | ÷ 1000 |

   Choose the card which makes the calculations correct.

   a) 36 _____ = 3.6   b) 45 _____ = 4500

   c) 2700 _____ = 2.7   d) 817 _____ = 81.7

   e) 0.99 _____ = 990   f) 860 _____ = 8.60

   g) 13.25 _____ = 132.5   h) 36.1 _____ = 3.61

5. Selina and Gemma were taking part in a swimathon. The swimming pool is 21m long.

   a) How far had Selina swam after she had completed 10 lengths?

   b) They swam a total of 100 lengths between them, how far did Selina and Gemma swim altogether?

   c) To change m into km you need to divide by 1000. How many km did Selina and Gemma swim altogether?

THE BASIC SKILLS - ADDING AND SUBTRACTING

NUMBER 5

You must not use a calculator.

1. Each side of these squares must add up to 20. Write in the missing numbers.

   a)
   ```
   | 5 | 8 |   |
   |   | ■ | 6 |
   | 9 | 4 |   |
   ```

   b)
   ```
   |   | 3 |   |
   | 7 | ■ | 5 |
   |   | 9 |   |
   ```

2. Find the answers to these adding chains.

   a) 1 + 2 + 3 + 4 + 5 = ☐

   b) 3 + 4 + 5 + 6 + 7 = ☐

3. Put rings around the two numbers which have a difference of 7.

   8   11   17   6   21   19   13   5

4. Fill in the missing numbers.

   a) 8 + 9 = ☐   b) 7 + ☐ = 11   c) ☐ + 6 = 8

   d) 19 − ☐ = 7   e) ☐ − 12 = 8   f) 12 − 8 = ☐

   g) ☐ + 13 = 19   h) 20 − ☐ = 4   i) 17 − 8 = ☐

5. Use these number cards to get the correct answers.

   7   14   20   4   5   13

   a) ☐ + ☐ + ☐ = 16

   b) ☐ − ☐ = ☐

   c) ☐ + ☐ − ☐ = 14

   d) ☐ + 8 = ☐ + ☐ + ☐

6. Fill in the missing numbers so that each side of these triangle adds up to 18.

   a) Top: 5, Bottom: 4, 8, ☐

   b) Top: ☐, Bottom-left pair: 4, 3; Bottom: ☐, 5, ☐

   c) Top: ☐, Right side: 1, 7; Bottom: ☐, 4, ☐

19/3/04

THE BASIC SKILLS - TIMES TABLES

NUMBER 6

You must not use a calculator.

1. Agent Muldoon has a secret code.

a	b	c	d	e	f	g	h	i	j	k	l	m
9	12	14	15	16	18	20	21	24	25	27	28	30

n	o	p	q	r	s	t	u	v	w	x	y	z
32	35	36	40	42	45	48	49	54	56	63	64	72

De-code this message. The first letter has been done for you.

6 x 4 = 24 **i**   8 x 6 = 48 **T**   5 x 9 = 45 **S**   9 x 4 = 36 **p**

3 x 3 = 9 **a**   6 x 7 = 42 **R**   6 x 8 = 48 **T**   8 x 8 = 64 **y**

8 x 6 = 48 **T**   3 x 8 = 24 **i**   6 x 5 = 30 **M**   4 x 4 = 16 **e**

I ATTRISTMpye

2. Find the cost of these sweets:

 7p EACH Chocolate Mice
 8p EACH Shoe Laces
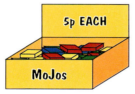 5p EACH MoJos
 4p EACH Cherry Lips
 6p EACH Jelly Beans

a) 5 chocolate mice — 35 p   b) 6 shoe laces — 48 p

c) 9 mojos — 45 p   d) 8 cherry lips — 32 p

e) 7 jelly beans — 42 p

f) How many shoe laces can be bought with 50p? 48 p

g) How many cherry lips can be bought with 30p? 24 p

3. In these shapes, the number in each square is found by multiplying the numbers in the circles on either side. Fill in the missing numbers.

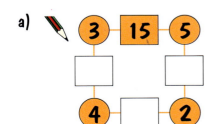
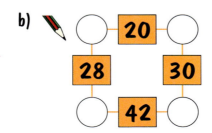
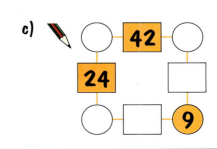

Key Stage 2 reference: Page 9   Science Revision Guides - The Essentials of Maths Key Stage 2

ADDING AND SUBTRACTING

NUMBER 7

1. Here is a list of numbers. Find which two numbers add up to 67 and put a ring around them.

   17   25   28   34   39   41   48

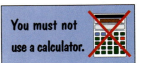
You must not use a calculator.

2. Here is another list of numbers. Find which three numbers next to each other add up to 14.1 and put a ring around them.

   4.3   4.4   4.5   4.6   4.7   4.8   4.9   5.0

3. Michael uses these number cards to make the sum: **3 4 5 6 7**

   6 3 7 + 4 5

   a) What is the answer to the sum that Michael has made? _____

   b) Use the cards to make this sum:

   ☐☐☐ + ☐☐ = 610

   c) Michael used his cards to make some subtractions. What is the answer to this subtraction?

   3 5 7 - 6 4 = _____

   d) How were the cards used to make this subtraction?

   ☐☐☐ - ☐☐ = 678

4. Write in the missing digits.

   a)   5 ☐ 7
      + ☐ 9 ☐
      ───────
        7 6 5

   b)   7 4 5
      − 2 ☐ 7
      ───────
        ☐ 9 ☐

   c)   ☐ 6 . ☐
      + 1 ☐ . 9
      ─────────
        7 4 . 3

   d)   3 . ☐
       − ☐ . 9 ☐
       ─────────
         1 . 6 4

MULTIPLYING

NUMBER 8

You must not use a calculator.

1. Mrs. Roberts wants to buy some prizes for her class.

   a) Find the cost of 6 Chocco bars.

   b) Find the cost of 25 cans of Cola.

2. Paper clips are sold in boxes which contain 144 paper clips each.

   a) How many paper clips are there in 12 boxes?

   b) How many paper clips are there in 35 boxes?

3. Imran uses these number cards to make this multiplication:

   a) What is the answer to Imran's multiplication?

   b) If Imran changed the cards around, what is the largest possible answer?

4. a) How much does it cost for 17 adults to go to the cinema?

   £

   CINEMA PRICES
   Adults £2.35
   Children £1.78

   b) How much does it cost for 63 children to go to the cinema?

   £

5. Fill in the missing digits:

   a) ☐ 2
      ×   7
      ─────
      4 3 ☐

   b) ☐ 7 ☐
      ×   8
      ─────
      2 1 8 4

   c) ☐ 2 3
      ×   6
      ─────
      2 5 3 ☐

Key Stage 2 reference: Page 11

DIVIDING

NUMBER 9

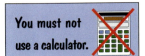
You must not use a calculator.

1. Calculate 456 ÷ 8.

2. A bag of 245 sweets is shared fairly between 7 children. How many sweets do they get each?

3. Calculate 598 ÷ 13.

4. 18 people share a prize of £486 equally between them. How much do they get each?

5. Work out 653 ÷ 17.

   rem.

6. 15 children share a bag of 576 sweets equally between them. How many sweets do they each get, and how many are left in the bag?

7. Put a ring around the correct answer to 546 ÷ 26.

      26   16   21   31   22   32

MORE DIVIDING

NUMBER 10

1. Calculate 9.84 ÷ 8.

   You must not use a calculator.

2. Find the missing number.

   a) 8 × ☐ = 288

   b) ☐ × 21 = 462

   c) 315 ÷ ☐ = 63

   d) 572 ÷ ☐ = 22

   e) ☐ ÷ 28 = 35

   f) ☐ ÷ 15 = 261

3. 264 children are going on a trip to the zoo. There needs to be at least 1 adult for every 15 children. How many adults need to go with the children?

4. Milk crates hold 24 bottles of milk each. A milkman needs to deliver 882 bottles of milk. How many crates of milk does he need?

5. Fill in the missing digits.

   a) 7☐
      4) 2 ☐ 2

   b) ☐ 4
      16) 3 8 ☐

   c) ☐ 7 ☐ ÷ 12 = 23

   d) 912 ÷ ☐ 8 = 24

THE NUMBER LINE

NUMBER 11

1. Mark the position of each of these numbers on the number line. The first one has been done for you.

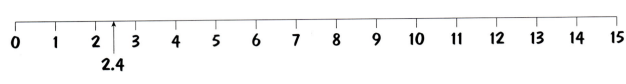

   a) 2.4   b) 6.5   c) 3.7   d) 12.23   e) 14.315   f) 9.023

2. Write in the boxes the numbers indicated by the arrows on this number line.

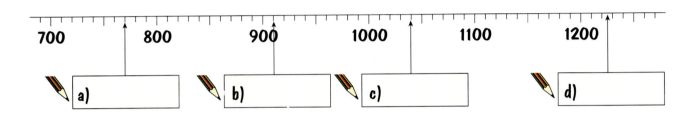

3. Write down the temperatures on these thermometers.

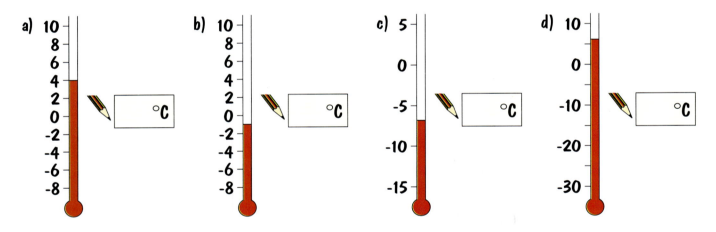

4. Write these temperatures in order, starting with the coldest.

   a)   -1°C   0.5°C   -2°C   5°C   -3.2°C

   [ ]   [ ]   [ ]   [ ]   [ ]

   b)   -11°C   -13°C   -8°C   -2°C   -9°C

   [ ]   [ ]   [ ]   [ ]   [ ]

5. Mark the position of each of these numbers on the number line.

   -11 -10 -9 -8 -7 -6 -5 -4 -3 -2 -1 0 1 2 3 4

   a) -3.4   b) 2.1   c) -5.7   d) -10.1   e) -8.25   f) -3.753

ADDING AND SUBTRACTING ON THE NUMBER LINE

NUMBER 12

1. Here are the midday temperatures in five cities on the same day in February.

London	1°C
Moscow	-17°C
Paris	-2°C
Oslo	-8°C
Cairo	27°C

a) Which city had the coldest temperature?

b) What is the difference between the temperature in London and Moscow?

c) What is the difference between the temperature in Paris and Oslo?

d) The temperature in Oslo had gone down by 5°C at midnight. What was the midnight temperature in Oslo?

2. Circle two numbers with a difference of 10.

    -6   -5   -4   -3   -2   -1   0   1   2   3   4   5

3. Look at these number cards.

    ⬚3⬚ ⬚5⬚ ⬚11⬚ ⬚15⬚ ⬚9⬚

a) Choose a card to give the answer -4.

   $\boxed{5} - \boxed{} = -4$

b) Choose a card to give the answer -2.

   $-11 + \boxed{} = -2$

c) Choose three different cards to give the answer -1.

   $\boxed{} - \boxed{} + \boxed{} = -1$

4. Use "+" or "−" signs to make these calculation correct.

a) $3 \boxed{} 7 = -4$

b) $-8 \boxed{} 12 = 4$

c) $3 \boxed{} 12 \boxed{} 2 = -7$

d) $14 \boxed{} 8 \boxed{} 19 = -13$

e) $-5 \boxed{} 17 \boxed{} 24 = -12$

f) $-18 \boxed{} 16 \boxed{} 12 = -22$

MULTIPLES, FACTORS AND PRIME NUMBERS

NUMBER 13

1. Here is a list of numbers:

       2   5   9   13   4   27

   a) Which of these numbers are multiples of 3? _____

   b) Which of these numbers are factors of 12? _____

   c) Which of these numbers are prime numbers? _____

2. a) Write down all the factors of 28.

   _____

   b) Which of these factors are prime numbers? _____

3. I think of a number.

   a) It is less than 20.
   It is not a prime number.
   It is an odd number.
   It is not a factor of 30.
   It is a multiple of 3.
   What number am I thinking of? _____

   b) It is less than 20.
   It is a prime number.
   It is a factor of 52.
   It is an odd number.
   What number am I thinking of? _____

4. a) Write down the first five multiples of 7.

   _____

   b) Which of these numbers are also factors of 63?

   _____

5. Kiran thinks that 39 is a prime number. Explain why Kiran is wrong.

   _____

SPECIAL NUMBERS

NUMBER 14

1. Jamie has some number cards.

   [2] [12] [4] [17] [9] [15]

   a) Which of these numbers are square numbers? ▢

   b) Two of these numbers add together to give a Cube Number. What are the two numbers and what is the cube number? ▢ + ▢ = ▢

2. Use a calculator to find:

   a) $\sqrt{324}$ ▢ b) $\sqrt{81}$ ▢

   c) $\sqrt{2.89}$ ▢ d) $\sqrt{42}$ ▢

3. A number multiplied by itself gives the answer 36. Circle the number.

   1 2 3 4 5 6 7 8 9

4. Lottery balls are numbered from 1 to 49.

   a) Which of these balls have square numbers on them?
   ▢

   b) Which of these balls have cube numbers on them?
   ▢

5. I think of a number between 40 and 90.

   It is a square number.

   It is an even number.

   What number am I thinking of? ▢

NUMBER PATTERNS

NUMBER 15

1. Write down the next number in these patterns.

   a) 2, 5, 8, 11, 14

   b) 2, 6, 18, 54

   c) 18, 13, 9, 6, 4

2. Here is a number pattern.

   1, 3, 6, 10. The rule for continuing this pattern is "Add 1 more each time."

   Write down the rule for each of these patterns.

   a) 2, 4, 6, 8, 10, 12

   b) 2, 4, 8, 16, 32, 64

   c) 2, 4, 7, 11, 16, 22

3. For each pattern below you are given the first two terms and the rule for continuing the pattern. Write down the next three terms.

   a) 1, 5,      Add 4 each time.

   b) 1, 5,      Multiply by 5 each time.

   c) 1, 5, 10   Add 1 more each time.

4. Abdul is trying to find the 25th term in this pattern:

   6, 12, 18, 24, 30 … He notices that term 1 is 6,

   term 2 is 12,

   term 3 is 18.

   So the rule is "multiply the term number by 6."

   The 25th term will be 25 × 6 = 150.

   a) Find the 75th term.

   b) Here is another pattern:

   8, 14, 20, 26, 32 …

   By comparing this pattern with the first one, write down the rule and find the 75th term.

   Rule: _____   75th term: _____

FORMULAS

NUMBER 16

1. **Nisha is making shapes out of black tiles.**

 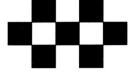 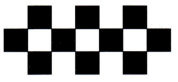 

Shape 1　　　Shape 2　　　　　Shape 3　　　　　　　Shape 4

Shape Number	1	2	3	4
Number of black tiles	4	7	10	13

How many black tiles will Nisha need for shape 5?

Nisha finds this formula for each shape:
   Number of Black Tiles = 3 × Shape number + 1.

Use Nisha's formula to find the number of black tiles she will need for:

a) Shape 5

b) Shape 9

c) Shape 20

2. **Joe uses his tiles to make these shapes:**

  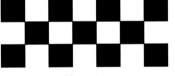 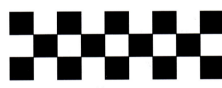

Shape 1　　　Shape 2　　　　　Shape 3　　　　　　　Shape 4

Shape Number (n)	1	2	3	4
Number of black tiles (t)	5	8	11	14

Joe writes his formula using letters: $t = 3n + 2$.

Use Joe's formula to find how many black tiles he will need for:

a) Shape 5

b) Shape 20

c) Shape 50

3. **Re-write these formulas using the letters in brackets.**

a) Number of tiles (t) = 4 × Shape number (n) − 2

b) Number of tiles (t) = 3 + Shape number (n) × 5

FRACTIONS

NUMBER 17

1. Shade in $\frac{1}{4}$ of this diagram.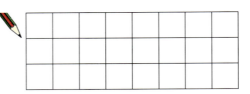

2. Draw a line joining any two shapes that have the same fraction shaded in.

   A 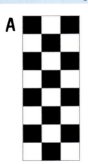   B 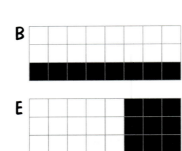   C 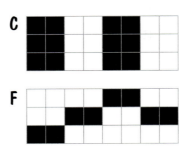   D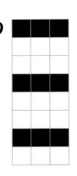

   E   F

3. a) Shade in $\frac{3}{4}$ of this circle.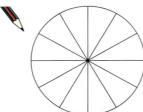

   b) Shade in $\frac{2}{3}$ of this circle.

   c) Which fraction is bigger $\frac{3}{4}$ or $\frac{2}{3}$?

4. a) Draw <u>one</u> line to join two fractions which have the same value.

   $\frac{2}{3}$

   $\frac{3}{4}$ $\frac{4}{5}$

   $\frac{5}{7}$ $\frac{6}{8}$

   $\frac{1}{2}$

   b) Explain how you know:

PERCENTAGES

NUMBER 18

1. Write in the missing numbers:

   a) $\dfrac{1}{\Box} = 50\%$

   b) $\dfrac{1}{4} = \Box\%$

   c) $\dfrac{\Box}{10} = 30\%$

   d) $\dfrac{4}{\Box} = 80\%$

   e) $\dfrac{8}{10} = \Box\%$

   f) $\dfrac{\Box}{\Box} = 75\%$

2. a) Shade $\tfrac{3}{5}$ of the shape below:

   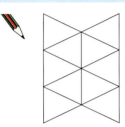

   b) What percentage of the shape have you shaded?

   ☐ %

3. Write these fractions as percentages:

   a) $\dfrac{5}{8} = $ ☐ %

   b) $\dfrac{2}{3} = $ ☐ %

   c) Which fraction is the biggest? ☐

4. Hayley went shopping in the sales for a coat.

   Coat A   Coat B   Coat C

   Coat A: SALE $\tfrac{1}{3}$ OFF
   Coat B: SALE 35% OFF
   Coat C: SALE $\tfrac{3}{8}$ OFF

   a) Write $\tfrac{1}{3}$ as a percentage. ☐ %

   b) Write $\tfrac{3}{8}$ as a percentage. ☐ %

   c) Which coat has the biggest reduction? ☐

5. Laura got $\tfrac{27}{40}$ in a maths test. Oliver got $\tfrac{35}{50}$ in a different maths test. Write each of these marks as a percentage and say who got the best mark.

   Laura ☐ %   Oliver ☐ %   Best mark ☐

Key Stage 2 reference: **Page 21**

FINDING A FRACTION AND A PERCENTAGE OF AN AMOUNT

NUMBER 19

1. Calculate the following:

   a) $\frac{1}{4}$ of 36p = ☐

   b) $\frac{2}{5}$ of 30p = ☐

   c) 10% of £30 = ☐

   d) 35% of 80m = ☐

2. The supermarket had two different boxes of cereal on special offer.

   Corn Flakes 500g — $\frac{1}{5}$ EXTRA

   Corn Crispies 500g — 25% EXTRA

   a) How many grams extra do you get if you buy the Corn Flakes? ☐ g

   b) How many grams extra do you get if you buy the Corn Crispies? ☐ g

3. a) Calculate 24% of £325.

   b) Calculate 62% of £525.

4. Fill in the missing numbers.

   a) $\frac{1}{2}$ of ☐ = 12

   b) $\frac{1}{4}$ of ☐ = 45

   c) $\frac{2}{3}$ of ☐ = 18

   d) 10% of ☐ = 27

   e) 40% of ☐ = 24

   f) 75% of ☐ = 36

5. Tom is 160cm tall, Harry is 80% of Tom's height and Mick's height is half way between Tom's and Harry's. How tall is Mick?

   ☐ cm

SOLVING PROBLEMS

NUMBER 20

1. Mrs. Roberts buys 9 drinks at 47p each and 6 drinks at 56p each. What is the total cost of the 15 drinks?

£ _____

2. a) A garden centre sells plants at £1.15 each. Find the cost of 25 plants.

£ _____

b) The garden centre also sells shrubs at £7 each. How many shrubs can be bought for £50?

_____

3. Abid buys one Dando, one Try and one Footy. He pays with a £1 coin. How much change will he get?

DANDO 24p | BANTIE 28p | TRY!! 33p | FOOTY 29p

_____ p

4. A machine makes 80000 drawing pins every day.

How many full boxes can be made from 80000 drawing pins? _____

5. A restaurant can seat up to 6 people around one table. How many tables are needed to seat 100 people?

_____

6. Tennis balls cost 45p each. How many tennis balls can be bought with a £20 note?

_____

ESTIMATING AND ROUNDING OFF

NUMBER 21

1. Stephen used his calculator to work out 1098 × £2.85. He said his answer was £11679.30. Use an estimate to check his answer and say if he is correct.

2. 7 friends agree to share a restaurant bill of £78.95 equally between them. Calculate how much they should pay to the nearest penny.

£ _____

3. A newspaper boy has to deliver 137 newspapers each weighing 165g. Estimate the total weight of newspapers.

_____ g

4. A piece of wood 234cm long has to be cut into 8 pieces of equal length. Calculate the length of each piece giving your answer to the nearest cm.

_____ cm

5. Mr. Shearer, the P.E. teacher, bought 12 new footballs for £57.60. Calculate the cost of each ball.

£ _____

6. Estimate the answer to each of the following:

a) £2.99 × 61   £ _____   b) 1.75kg + 4.19kg + 2.81kg   _____ kg

c) £585 ÷ 19   £ _____   d) £400 − £53.11 − £48.19   £ _____

CO-ORDINATES

NUMBER 22

1. Point A has co-ordinates (4, 7). Write down the co-ordinates of the other points.

   Point B (,)

   Point C (,)

   Point D (,)

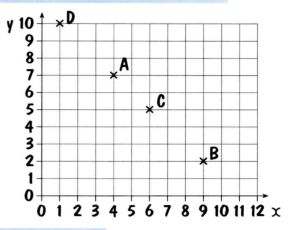

2. Plot these points on the grid, joining them up as you go along.

   (5, 1) (7, 1) (9, 3) (9, 5) (7, 7)

   (5, 7) (3, 5) (3, 3) (5, 1)

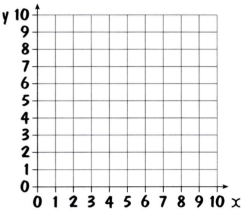

3. The crosses on the line are equally spaced.

   a) What are the co-ordinates of point A?

   (,)

   b) What are the co-ordinates of point B?

   (,)

   c) If the line was made longer, would the point with co-ordinates (10, 15) be on the line? Explain your answer.

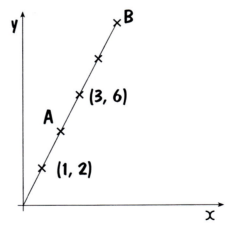

4. Fill in the missing co-ordinates.

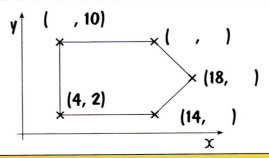

Key Stage 2 reference: **Page 25** Science Revision Guides - **The Essentials of Maths Key Stage 2**

DESCRIBING SHAPES

SHAPE, SPACE & MEASURE 1

1. Here are some shapes:

A   B   C   D   E   F

a) Which shape has only one pair of parallel sides and is a quadrilateral?

b) What sort of polygon is shape E?

c) Which shape is not a polygon?

d) Which shape has the most pairs of parallel sides?

2. Here are 8 polygons:

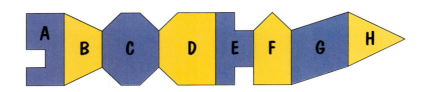

A B C D E F G H

a) Which of these polygons are quadrilaterals?

b) What sort of polygon is shape H?

c) Which of these polygons are pentagons?

d) Which of these polygons are hexagons?

e) Which of these polygons are octagons?

3. On the grid below, draw:

a) A hexagon with only one pair of parallel sides.

b) A regular quadrilateral.

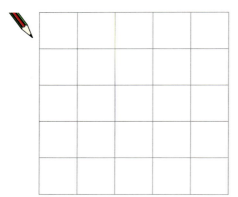 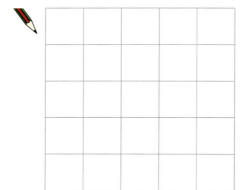

The Essentials of **MATHS** Key Stage Two **Pupil Worksheets**   **ANSWERS**

These answers have been deliberately put in the middle of the book so that they can be easily taken out if you don't want to be able to see them. If you do use them, use them wisely. Check your answers are correct, and then do any corrections for any wrong answers. If you are totally stuck read the answers and see if you can work out how to get the correct answer. If you just copy the answers down, the only person you are cheating is yourself. For some questions, there is more than one possible answer, these are marked with an *.

NUMBER

Page 2   **1.** 203 3 units, 3417 3 thousands, 4329 3 hundreds, 26.35 3 tenths, 18.13 3 hundredths
2. a) 76 b) 306 c) 7630 d) 3067   **3.** a) 9876 b) 0.123   **4.** a) 1863 or 1836 b) 6813 or 6831

Page 3   **1.** 4, 15, 17, 28, 29, 38   **2.** 137, 173, 317, 371, 713, 731   **3.** 258, 285, 528, 582, 825, 852
4. a) 2.29, 2.37, 2.45, 2.58 b) 5.76, 5.79, 5.8, 6.0 c) 4.723, 47.23, 472.3, 4723
d) 0.03, 0.1, 0.13, 0.3, 0.31   **5.** 2.1, 2.2, 2.3, 2.4, 2.5, 2.6 *

Page 4   **1.** 350 ÷ 10 35, 35 x 100 3500, 35 x 10 350, 3500 ÷ 100 35   **2.** 8050
3. a) 630 b) 150 c) 820 d) 10 e) 24 f) 100 g) 5000 h) 360.   **4.** a) 620 ÷ 10 = 62*
b) 51 x 10 = 510* c) 47 x 10 = 470* d) 62 x 100 = 6200*   **5.** a) 800m b) 3300m c) 52
6. a) 70 b) 1500 c) 100

Page 5   **1.** a) three b) two, right c) one, left   **2.** 35   **3.** 87000   **4.** a) ÷ 10 b) x 100 c) ÷ 1000
d) ÷10 e) x 1000 f) ÷ 100 g) x 10 h) ÷ 10   **5.** a) 210m b) 2100m c) 2.1 km

Page 6   **1.** a) | 5 | 8 | 7 | b) | 9 | 3 | 8 | **2.** a) 15 b) 25   **3.** 6, 13   **4.** a) 17 b) 4 c) 2 d) 12 e) 20 f) 4
| 6 | ■ | 6 | | 7 | ■ | 5 | g) 6 h) 16 i) 9
| 9 | 4 | 7 | | 4 | 9 | 7 |
5. a) 4 + 5 + 7 b) 20 - 13 = 7* c) 13 + 5 - 4 d) 14 + 8 = 13 + 5 + 4   **6.** a) 5   b) 8   c) 7
                                                                                              9 7   4 3   1 7
                                                                                              4 8 6   6 5 7   10 4 4

Page 7   **1.** Its party time   **2.** a) 35p b) 48p c) 45p d) 32p e) 42p f) 6 g) 7
3. a) 12 8 10 b) 4 5 c) 6   7
                          7 6   4 36 63

Page 8   **1.** 28 + 39   **2.** 4.6 + 4.7 + 4.8   **3.** a) 682 b) 547 + 63* c) 293 d) 734 - 56
4. a) 567 + 198 b) 745 - 247 = 498 c) 56.4 + 17.9 d) 3.6 - 1.96

Page 9   **1.** a) £2.22 or 222p b) £7 or 700p   **2.** a) 1728 b) 5040   **3.** a) 24702 b) 48295 (743 x 65)
4. a) £39.95 b) £112.14   **5.** a) 62 x 7 = 434 b) 273 x 8 = 2184 c) 423 x 6 = 2538

Page 10   **1.** 57   **2.** 35   **3.** 46   **4.** £27   **5.** 38 rem 7   **6.** 38 rem 6   **7.** 21

Page 11   **1.** 1.23   **2.** a) 36 b) 22 c) 5 d) 26 e) 980 f) 3915   **3.** 18   **4.** 37
5. a) 292 ÷ 4 = 73 b) 384 ÷ 16 = 24 c) 276 ÷ 12 = 23 d) 912 ÷ 38 = 24

Page 12   **1.** number line 0 to 15 with marks at 3.7, 6.5, 9.023, 12.23, 14.315   **2.** a) 770 b) 910 c) 1040 d) 1225
3. a) 4°c b) -1°c c) -7°c d) 6°c   **4.** a) -3.2°c, -2°c, -1°c, 0.5°c, 5°c b) -13°c, -11°c, -9°c, -8°c, -2°c
5. number line from -11 to 4 with marks at -10.1, -8.25, -5.7, -3.753, -3.4, 2.1

Page 13   **1.** a) Moscow b) 18°c c) 6°c d) -13°c   **2.** -6, 4 or -5,5   **3.** a) 9 b) 9 c) 9 - 15 + 5 = 1
4. a) -   b) +   c) -,+   d) -,-   e) +,-   f) -, +

NUMBER — ANSWERS

Page 14 1. a) 9, 27 b) 2, 4 c) 2, 5, 13   2. a) 1, 2, 4, 7, 14, 28 b) 2, 7   3. a) 9 b) 13
4. a) 7, 14, 21, 28, 35 b) 7, 21   5. Because 3 x 13 = 39*

Page 15 1. a) 4, 9 b) 12 + 15 = 27   2. a) 18 b) 9 c) 1.7 d) 6.48   3. 6
4. a) 1, 4, 9, 16, 25, 36, 49 b) 1, 8, 27   5. 64

Page 16 1. a) 17 b) 162 c) 3   2. a) Add 2 each time b) Times by 2 each time c) Add 1 more each time
3. a) 9, 13, 17 b) 25, 125, 625 c) 16, 23, 31   4. a) 450 b) Multiply the term number by 6 then add 2, 452

Page 17 1. 16 a) 16 b) 28 c) 61   2. a) 17 b) 62 c) 152   3. a) t = 4n - 2 b) t = 3 + 5n*

Page 18 1. Any 6 squares shaded in   2. A↔C, B↔F, D↔E   3. a) Any 9 sectors shaded
b) Any 8 sectors shaded   c) $\frac{3}{4}$ 4. a) $\frac{3}{4} \leftrightarrow \frac{6}{8}$ b) $\frac{1}{4} = \frac{2}{8}$ so $\frac{3}{4} = \frac{6}{8}$ *

Page 19 1. a) 2 b) 25 c) 3 d) 5 e) 80 f) $\frac{3}{4}$ 2. a) Any 6 triangles shaded b) 60%   3. a) 62.5% b) 66.7%
c) $\frac{2}{3}$ 4. a) 33.3% b) 37.5% c) Coat C   5. Laura 67.5%, Oliver 70%. Best mark Oliver

Page 20 1. a) 9p b) 12p c) £3 d) 28m   2. a) 100g b) 125g   3. a) £78 b) £325.50
4. a) 24 b) 180 c) 27 d) 270 e) 60 f) 48   5. 144cm

Page 21 1. £7.59   2. a) £28.75 b) 7   3. 14p   4. 533   5. 17   6. 44

Page 22 1. 1000 x £3 = £3000. Stephen is wrong   2. £11.28   3. 100 x 200 = 20000g   4. 29cm
5. £4.80   6. a) £180 b) 9kg c) £30 d) £300

Page 23 1. B(9,2), C(6,5), D(1,10)
3. a) (2,4) b) (5,10) c) No. because the y-coordinate is not twice the x-coordinate.
4. (4,10), (14,10), (18,6), (14,2)

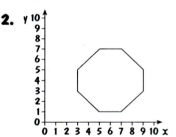

SHAPE, SPACE AND MEASURE

Page 24 1. a) A b) Pentagon c) F d) D   2. a) B, G b) Triangle c) F d) D e) A, E, C
3. a) * b)

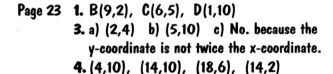

Page 29 1. a) C b) B, E c) All the sides are the same length, and all the angles are the same size.
2. a) C b) E c) D d) A e) B, rectangles   3.

Page 30 1. a) Obtuse b) Acute c) Right d) Reflex   2. a) 4 b) 45° c) 10   3. a) A, C b) B, D c) D, E
4. a)   b)

Page 31 1. a) A = 65°, B = 57°, C = 58° b) D = 66°, E = 104°, F = 68°, G = 122° (You may be 1° different)
2. 4.4 to 4.6cm

SHAPE, SPACE AND MEASURE

ANSWERS

Page 32 1.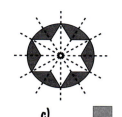

2. a) 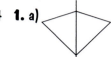   b)   c)   3. STOP

Page 33 1. Size, Shape   2. A and D   3. B   4. Six arrow heads added

Page 34 1. a)   b) 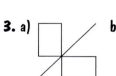   2. a)   b)   3. a) 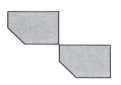   b)

Page 35 1. a) Translation   b) Reflection   c) Rotation
2. a)   b)    3. a)   b)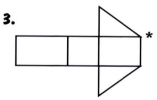

Page 36 1. B and D   2. B and C   3.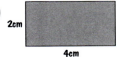

Page 37 1. a) 3.5cm, 4.5cm, 5cm   b) 44mm, .47mm, 63mm   2. a) 115cm   b) 110cm   c) 97cm
3. a) 1.23km   b) 1360m   c) 1.6km   4. 75cm   5. 4.76m 4.94m 5.07m 5.21m

Page 38 1. a) 2400kg b) 2.4t   2. 9.1kg   3. a) 1300g   b) 1180g   c) 1290g
4. a) 6.4kg   b) 1.7kg   c) 12kg   d) 90g   e) 260g   f) 2.3kg   g) 47g

Page 39 1. 0.568l   2. 2200cm^3 3. 25cm^3 4. a) 1100ml   b) 0.75l   c) 65cm^3 d) 3.6ml   e) 460ml
5. Line at 0.7

Page 40 1. a) (i) 120s   (ii) 210s   (iii) 285s   b) (i) 180mins   (ii) $2\frac{1}{2}$ mins   (iii) 75 mins   c) (i) 7 hrs   (ii) 48 hrs
(iii) 60 hrs   2. a) 4 days   b) 100 miles   3. a) 3 hrs 10 mins   b) 1 hr 20 mins   c) 9 hrs 45 mins
d) 5 hrs 20 mins   4. a) 0840, 1505   b) 6 hrs 25 mins   5. 8.25   6. 2hrs 45 mins

Page 41 1. a) more   b) less   c) less   d) less   e) more   f) less   2. a) 3kg   b) 8kg   c) 30kg   d) 20 cm   e) 80 in
f) 10 inches   g) 4m   h) 80 inches   i) 1 yard   j) 5 pints   k) 16l   l) 40l   3. 21 or 22   4. About 9.5 s
because 100 yards is a bit less than 100m.
1. a) 2m   b) 3 or 4m   c) 10 to 15m   d) 200m *   2. a) 100   b) 2.5kg   3. 60 - 70ml, 60 - 70g

Page 42 1. a)   b)   2. a) 24cm   b) 26m   c) 22cm   d) 34m

3. a) about 12.1cm   b) about 9.6cm   4. a) 40cm   b) 64cm

Page 43 1. a) 12cm² b) 12cm² 2. a)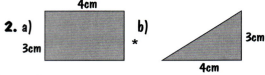

3. a) 2cm² b)   c) 12cm²

Page 44 1. a) 12cm³ b) 18cm³ 2. a) 10cm³ b) 36m³ 3. a) 10 boxes b) 90cm³

HANDLING DATA

Page 45 1. a)

Frequency
11
3
15
6
TOTAL = 35

b) car c) 35 2. a)

Number of Grapes	Tally	Frequency
20 - 24	JHT I	6
25 - 29	JHT JHT JHT II	17
30 - 34	JHT JHT II	12
35 - 39	JHT	5
		TOTAL = 40

b) 29

Page 46 1. a) 16 b) 19 c) He could be wrong because one person could own all the tropical fish.
2. 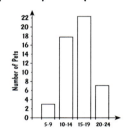   3. a) 15 b) 23 c) 7

2.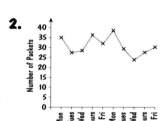

Page 47 1. a) 6 b) 39 c) Tuesday
3. a) about $\frac{1}{8}$ b) £200 c) about £300 d) about £50

Page 48 1. a) 3 b) 24 c) Monday   2. a) 45 miles b) 170 miles c) 307 miles d) 28 miles
3. a) 1330 b) 31 minutes c) 1146

Page 49 1. a) 48.1 b) 48 c) 48   2. a) 13 b) 19.13 c) 20 d) 20 3. a) 4.9 b) 30.6 c) 30.22
4. 12, 14, 16, 16, 17   5. a) 10 b) 0.5

Page 50 1. C D A E B   2. 0, 0.2, 0.5, $\frac{3}{6}$, $\frac{3}{4}$, 1   3. a) $\frac{1}{5}$ to $\frac{1}{2}$ b) 0 c) 0.1
d) 0.001 or smaller   4. She must be wrong as a probability cannot be more than 1

Page 51 1. a) $\frac{3}{10}$ b) $\frac{4}{10}$ c) 0   2. a) $\frac{1}{6}$ b) $\frac{3}{6}$ or $\frac{1}{2}$ c) $\frac{4}{6}$ or $\frac{2}{3}$
3. a) $\frac{1}{4}$ b) $\frac{1}{8}$ c) B d) Equally likely   4. a) [spinner with 4,1,2,1,1,2,3,1] b) $\frac{2}{8}$ or $\frac{1}{4}$

Page 52 1. a) $\frac{1}{6}$ b) $\frac{2}{6}$ or $\frac{1}{3}$ c) $\frac{3}{6}$ or $\frac{1}{2}$ 2. a)

First Sock	Second Sock
Red	Red
Red	Blue
Blue	Red
Blue	Blue

b) $\frac{1}{4}$ c) $\frac{2}{4}$ or $\frac{1}{2}$

3. a) 3 b) 8 c) $\frac{4}{24}$ or $\frac{1}{6}$ d) $\frac{10}{24}$ or $\frac{5}{12}$

Page 53 1. a) $\frac{3}{10}$ b) 0 c) $\frac{27}{100}$ d) $\frac{17}{100}$ e) the second set, because the experiment has been repeated a lot more times.
2. a) B b) A c) B d) A

TRIANGLES, QUADRILATERALS AND 3-D SHAPES

SHAPE, SPACE & MEASURE 2

1. Here are some triangles:

a) Which triangle is an equilateral triangle?

b) Which two triangles are isosceles triangles?

c) What makes the equilateral triangle different from the other triangles?

2. Rachel received these parcels for her birthday.

 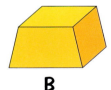

A   B   C   D   E

Which parcel fits the following description?

a) Parcel ____ has three faces, one is curved and the other two are circles.

b) Parcel ____ has five corners (vertices) and one square face.

c) Parcel ____ has one curved face and one circular face.

d) Parcel ____ has twelve edges that are all the same length.

e) Parcel ____ has six faces, two are trapeziums, the other four are ____ (fill in the missing word)

3. The fundamental property of a parallelogram is that "both pairs of opposite sides are parallel." Put a tick in the three shapes that are special parallelograms.

ANGLES

SHAPE, SPACE & MEASURE 3

1. Choose the correct word from the list to make the sentences correct.

   | Right | Isosceles | Acute | Radius | Reflex | Obtuse | Degree |

   a) An angle that is between 90° and 180° is called an _____ angle.

   b) An angle that is less than 90° is called an _____ angle.

   c) A 90° angle is called a _____ angle.

   d) An angle that is between 180° and 360° is called a _____ angle.

2. This pointer starts at 0 and turns in a clockwise direction.

   a) What number does it point to after a turn of 90°? _____

   b) What angle does it turn going from 0 to 2? _____

   c) What number does it point to after a turn of 225°? _____

3. Here are some shapes ...

   A   B   C   D   E

   a) Which shapes have two acute and two obtuse angles? _____

   b) Which shapes have two right angles? _____

   c) Which shapes have not got any acute angles? _____

4. Use the grid below to draw:

   a) A pentagon with three right angles.   b) A hexagon with three right angles.

      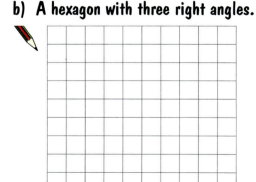

MEASURING AND DRAWING ANGLES

SHAPE, SPACE & MEASURE 4

1. Measure all the angles in each shape.

a)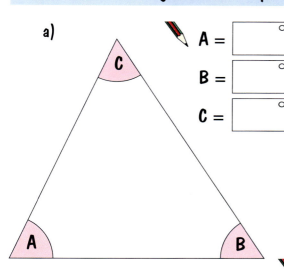

A = ☐°
B = ☐°
C = ☐°

b)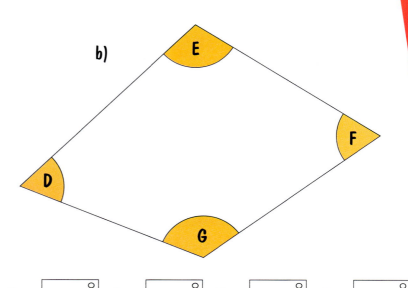

D = ☐° E = ☐° F = ☐° G = ☐°

2. Here is a rough sketch of a kite.

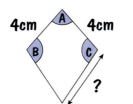

A = 80°
B = 105°
C = 105°

Make an accurate full size drawing of the kite and measure the length of the side marked with a "?". The first line has been drawn for you.

side marked ? = ☐ cm

SYMMETRY

SHAPE, SPACE & MEASURE 5

1. Year 6 have made some designs for a new school badge.

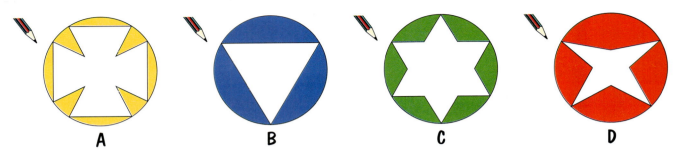

For each badge draw a dotted line to show each line of symmetry.

2. a) Shade in one more square so that the shape has rotational symmetry of order 2.

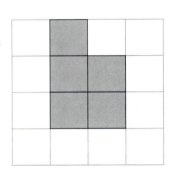

b) Shade in two more squares so that the dotted line is a line of symmetry.

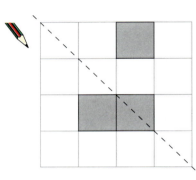

c) Shade in seven more squares to make a shape that has rotational symmetry of order 4, but no lines of symmetry.

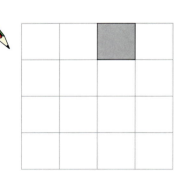

3. A motorist looks in the mirror and sees this sign on the car behind.

Write down what the message says.

CONGRUENT SHAPES

SHAPE, SPACE & MEASURE 6

1. Fill in the missing words:

   Two shapes are congruent if they are exactly the same [   ] and [   ]

2. Which two kites below are congruent?

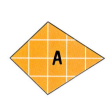 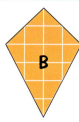  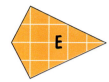

   Shapes [   ] and [   ] are congruent.

3. Which one of the shapes below has been cut out of the piece of cardboard?

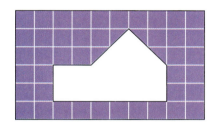 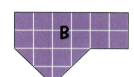 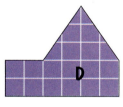

   [   ]

4. This shape is called an "arrowhead." Add six more "arrowheads" to the pattern below.

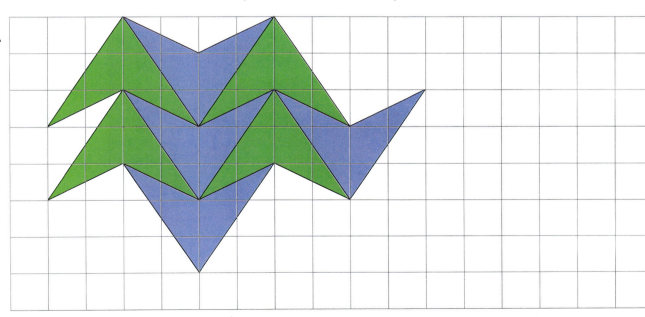

TRANSFORMATIONS - REFLECTION

SHAPE, SPACE & MEASURE 7

1. Draw the reflection of each triangle in the mirror line.

a)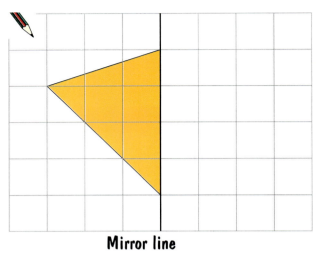
Mirror line

b)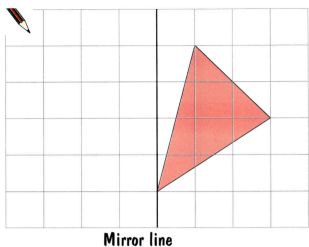
Mirror line

2. Draw the reflection of each shape in the mirror line.

a)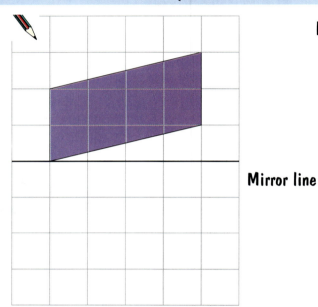
Mirror line

b)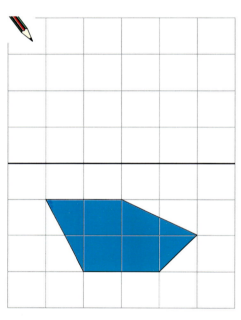
Mirror line

3. Draw the reflection of each shape in the mirror line.

a)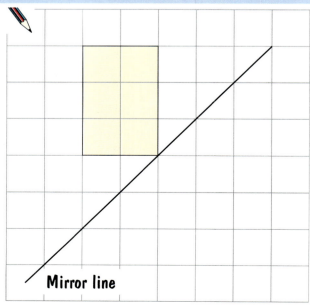
Mirror line

b)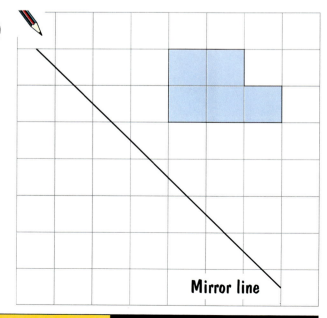
Mirror line

TRANSLATIONS AND ROTATIONS

SHAPE, SPACE & MEASURE 8

1. Choose the correct type of transformation from REFLECTION, TRANSLATION, ROTATION and write it in the box to make these sentences correct:

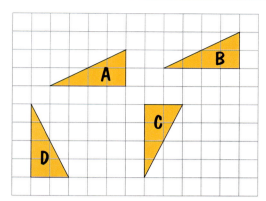

a) Triangle B is a [ ] of triangle A.

b) Triangle C is a [ ] of triangle A.

c) Triangle D is a [ ] of triangle A.

2. a) Translate this rectangle four places right and three places up.

b) Translate this shape three places left and two places up.

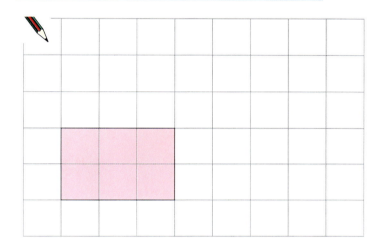

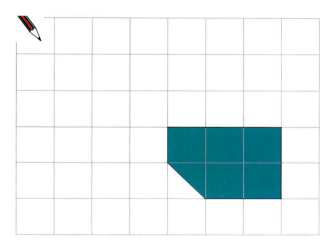

3. a) Turn this shape through one right angle in a clockwise direction around point C. Draw its new position.

b) Rotate this shape 90° in an anti-clockwise direction about point D. Draw its new position.

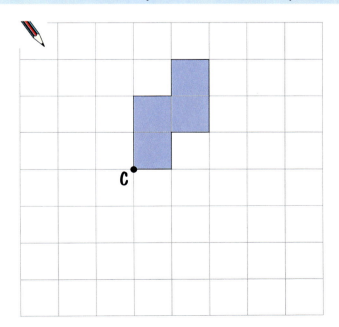

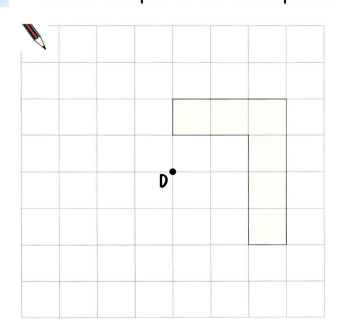

Key Stage 2 reference: Page 37 — Science Revision Guides - The Essentials of Maths Key Stage 2

MAKING 3-D MODELS

SHAPE, SPACE & MEASURE 9

1. Which of these nets DO NOT make a cube?

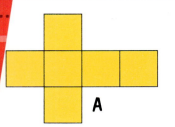 A
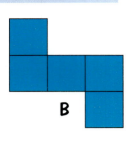 B
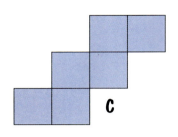 C
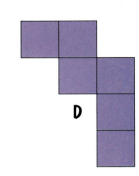 D

 do not make a cube.

2. Which of these nets would make the box shown?

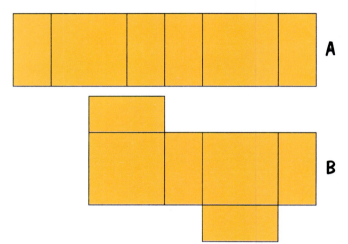
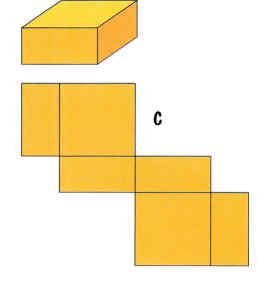

A, B, C

 would make the box.

3. Dale is designing a special box to display a gift. He wants to make a box with a lid that looks like this:

He is drawing a sketch of the net, it does not have to be the right size, but it needs to be neat. Finish the sketch for him.

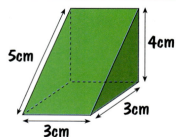

LENGTH

SHAPE, SPACE & MEASURE 10

1. Measure the length of each side of these triangles. Give your answer as accurately as you can.

a) Give your answer in centimetres.

b) Give your answer in millimetres.

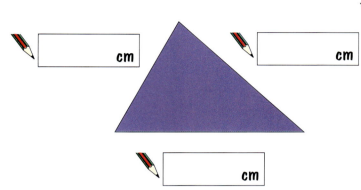
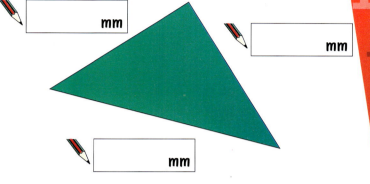

2. In a high jump competition ...

a) Mario jumped 1.15m, how many centimetres is this? ____ cm

b) Huw jumped 1.1m, how many centimetres is this? ____ cm

c) Wally jumped 0.97m, how many centimetres is this? ____ cm

3. James, Lynda and Bruce had a competition to see how far they could run in ten minutes.

a) James ran 1230m, how far is this in kilometres? ____ km

b) Lynda ran 1.36km, how far is this in metres? ____ m

c) Bruce ran 1600m, how far is this in kilometres? ____ km

4. Grace had her height measured when she was 18 months old. How tall is Grace?

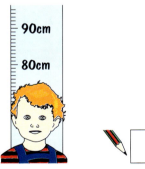

____ cm

5. In a cricket ball throwing competition, flags were placed where the balls landed, and then a tape measure was used to measure the distance thrown. Write down how far each ball was thrown.

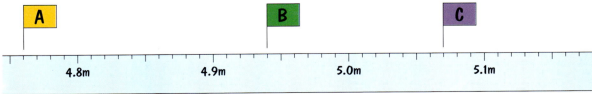

A = ____ m   B = ____ m   C = ____ m   D = ____ m

MASS

SHAPE, SPACE & MEASURE — 11

1. Coal is sold in 50kg sacks. A lorry has 48 sacks of coal on it.

   a) What is the mass of forty eight 50kg sacks in kg? _____ kg

   b) How many tonnes is this? _____ t

2. Maisy puts 5g of sugar in her cup of tea. She has five cups a day, seven days a week for fifty two weeks a year. So in one year she has 5 × 5 × 7 × 52 = 9100g of sugar in her tea.

   How many kg is this? _____ kg

3. A vet in a zoo measured the mass of three baby chimpanzees.

   They were a) 1.3kg b) 1.18kg and c) 1.29kg. Write each of these in grams.

   a) _____ g   b) _____ g   c) _____ g

4. What mass do each of these scales show?

   a)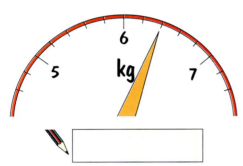

   b)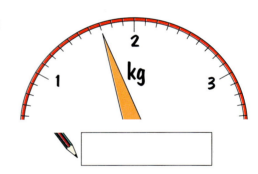

   c)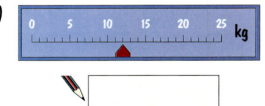

   d)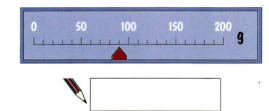

   e)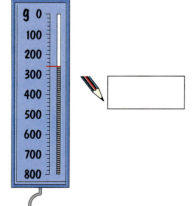

   f)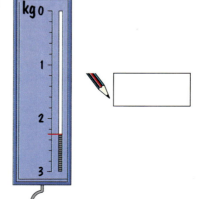

   g)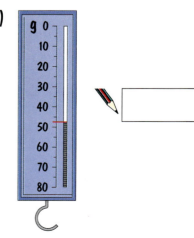

CAPACITY

SHAPE, SPACE & MEASURE | 12

1. A milk bottle holds 568 ml of milk.

   Write 568ml in litres.  L

2. A car engine has a capacity of 2.2 litres.

   Write 2.2 litres in cm^3.  cm^3

3. A tablespoon holds 25 ml of sugar.

   Write 25 ml in cm^3.  cm^3

4. How much water is in each of these containers?

   a) 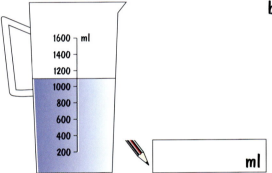 ml

   b) 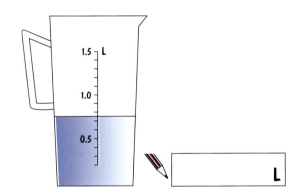 L

   c) 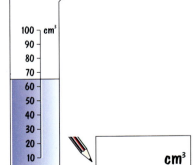 cm^3

   d) 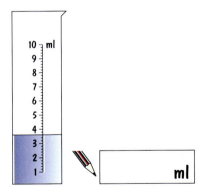 ml

   e) 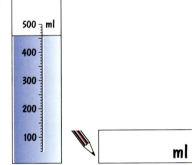 ml

5. Sabrina has to measure 700 ml of milk in this jug. Draw a line to show where the milk should go up to.

   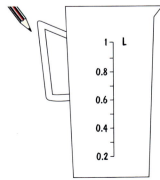

TIME

SHAPE, SPACE & MEASURE 13

1. a) How many seconds are there in:

   i) 2 minutes [___] s ii) 3½ minutes [___] s iii) 4¾ minutes [___] s

   b) How many minutes are there in:

   i) 3 hours [___] mins ii) 150 seconds [___] mins iii) 1¼ hours [___] mins

   c) How many hours are there in:

   i) 420 minutes [___] hrs ii) 2 days [___] hrs iii) 2½ days [___] hrs

2. Three friends are planning a sponsored bike ride. They are hoping to cycle 400 miles in 96 hours.

   a) How many days is 96 hours? [___] days

   b) How many miles a day on average is this? [___] miles

3. How long is it from:

   a) 8.30am to 11.40am? [___]   b) 11.45am to 1.05pm? [___]

   c) 9.30pm to 7.15am? [___]   c) 1350 to 1910? [___]

4. The school day starts at 8.40am and finishes at 3.05pm.

   a) Write these times in 24 hour clock time:

   Starts: [___]   Finishes: [___]

   b) How long is the school day? [___]

5. A television programme starts at 7.40 and lasts for 45 minutes.

   At what time does it finish? [___]

6. A concert started at 8.30 and finished at 11.15.

   How long did the concert last for? [___]

IMPERIAL UNITS

SHAPE, SPACE & MEASURE 14

1. Use the words "more" or "less" to complete the following statements.
   a) 3m is a bit [ ] than 3 yards.
   b) 8 yards is a bit [ ] than 8m.
   c) 20lb is a bit [ ] than 10kg.
   d) 1kg is a bit [ ] than 3lb.
   e) 18 pints is a bit [ ] than 9 litres.
   f) 12 litres is a bit [ ] than 24 pints.

2. Which is the bigger? Put a ring around your answer.
   a) 3kg or 6lbs.
   b) 8kg or 4lbs.
   c) 50lbs or 30kg.
   d) 6 inches or 20cm.
   e) 80cm or 80 inches.
   f) 5cm or 10 inches.
   g) 4m or 4 yards.
   h) 1m or 80 inches.
   i) 50cm or 1 yard.
   j) 2 litres or 5 pints.
   k) 8 pints or 16 litres.
   l) 40 litres or 60 pints.

3. A cardboard box can safely hold up to 10kg without breaking. How many 1lb jars of jam can be safely carried in the box? [ ] jars of jam.

4. Donovan Bailey ran 100m in 9.84 seconds, setting a new world record. Estimate how long you think it would take him to run 100 yards. Explain your answer.

ESTIMATING MEASURES

1. An adult is about 1.8m high.
   a) Estimate the height of a classroom door. [ ] m
   b) Estimate the height of a room in your house. [ ] m
   c) Estimate the height of a house. [ ] m
   d) A skyscraper has 52 floors. Estimate its height. [ ] m

2. 4 large potatoes weigh about 1kg.
   a) Estimate how many potatoes there will be in a 25kg sack. [ ] potatoes
   b) 10 potatoes are in a bag, estimate their mass [ ] kg

3. 1 litre of lemonade weighs about 1kg. About 15 glasses can be poured from a 1 litre bottle. Estimate the capacity of each glass and the mass of lemonade in each glass.

Key Stage 2 reference: Page 43 Science Revision Guides - The Essentials of Maths Key Stage 2

PERIMETER

SHAPE, SPACE & MEASURE 15

1. On the grid below draw a rectangle with a perimeter of ...

   a) 12cm

   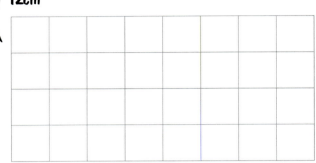

   b) 10cm

   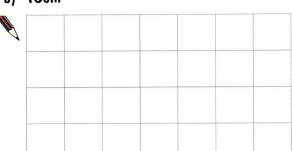

2. Find the perimeter of each of these shapes.

   a) 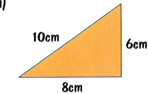 ☐ cm

   b)  ☐ m

   c) 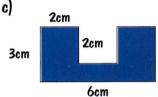 ☐ cm

   d) 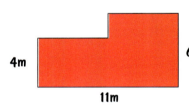  ☐ m

3. By measuring accurately find the perimeter of these shapes:

   a) 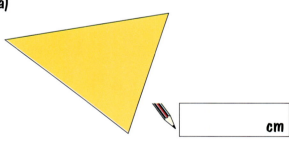 ☐ cm

   b)  ☐ cm

4. Rashid is making loops out of regular octagons. Each edge is 2cm.

   Find the length of the outer edge of each loop.

   a) 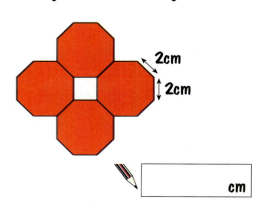 ☐ cm

   b) 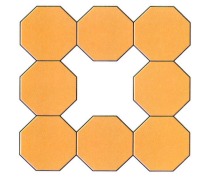 ☐ cm

AREA

SHAPE, SPACE & MEASURE 16

1. The area of each square on the grid is 1cm². What is the area of these shapes?

   a)
   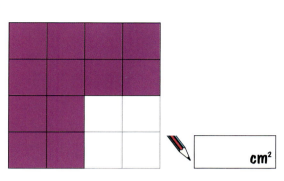
   ___ cm²

   b)
   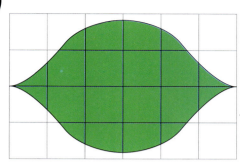
   ___ cm²

2. a) On the grid below draw a rectangle with an area of 12cm².

   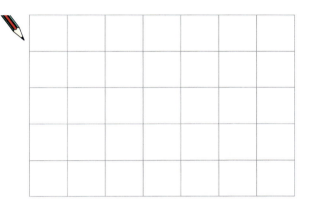

   b) On the grid below draw a triangle with an area of 6cm².

   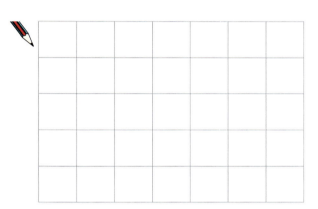

3. This square has an area of 1cm².

   So these triangles have an area of $\frac{1}{2}$ cm² each.

   Four of these triangles make this square.

   a) What is the area of this square? ___ cm²

   b) Draw a square with an area of 8cm² on this grid.

   c) What is the area of this rectangle?

   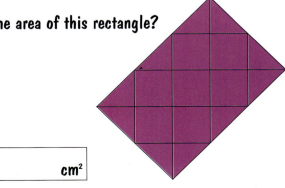

   ___ cm²

VOLUME

SHAPE, SPACE & MEASURE 17

1. These shapes are made from 1cm³ cubes. Find the volume of each shape.

   a) 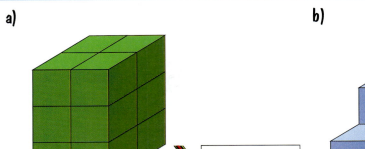 ___ cm³

   b) 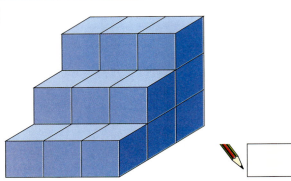 ___ cm³

2. Emily has some building bricks.

   These bricks have a volume of 2cm³.

   These bricks have a volume of 1cm³.

   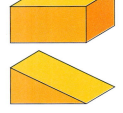

   She uses the bricks to build some towers. Find the volume of each tower.

   a) 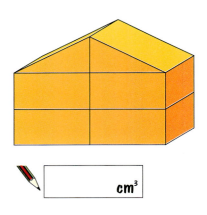 ___ cm³

   b) 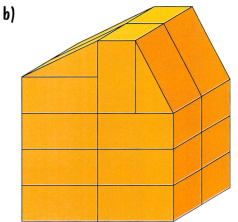 ___ cm³

3. Each of these boxes have a volume of 9cm³.

   a) What is the largest number of these boxes that can fit in the tray.

   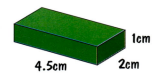

   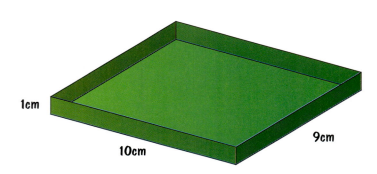

   ___ boxes

   b) What is the volume of the tray?  ___ cm³

COLLECTING DATA

HANDLING DATA 1

1. Andrew did a survey of how the children in his class got to school. He collected this data in a tally chart.

   a) Fill in the frequency column.

Method	Tally	Frequency
Walk	IIII IIII I	
Cycle	III	
Car	IIII IIII IIII	
Bus	IIII I	
	TOTAL =	

   b) What was the most common way of getting to school?

   c) How many children are there in Andrew's class?

2. A greengrocer counted the number of grapes in 40 bunches. She recorded the number of grapes in each bunch in a list.

   28 35 21 29 27 33 26 28 37 29

   30 32 36 24 31 30 38 22 25 27

   31 33 29 34 26 28 24 31 28 26

   32 30 28 35 33 29 27 20 26 22

   a) Put these amounts in the tally chart below.

Number of Grapes	Tally	Frequency
20 - 24		
25 - 29		
30 - 34		
35 - 39		
	TOTAL =	

   b) How many bunches had between 25 and 34 grapes on them?

Key Stage 2 reference: **Page 47**   Science Revision Guides - **The Essentials of Maths Key Stage 2**   45

BAR CHARTS AND PICTOGRAMS

HANDLING DATA 2

1. Gary drew this bar chart to display the results of his survey on children's pets. Each bar shows the number of each type of pet.

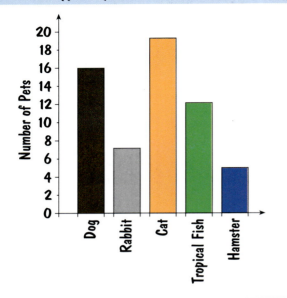

a) How many pets are dogs?

b) How many pets are cats?

c) Gary says that more people have tropical fish than rabbits. Could he be wrong? Explain your answer.

2. Michaela counted the number of chips people got with their dinners.

Number of chips	5 - 9	10 - 14	15 - 19	20 - 24
Number of people	3	18	22	7

Complete Michaela's bar chart for her.

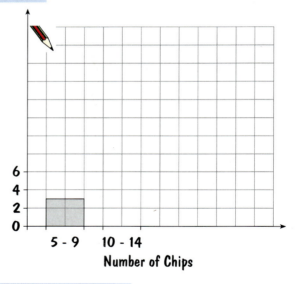

3. Salim displayed the results of his survey on people's pocket money in a pictogram.

Amount of pocket money	Number of People
£1.00 to £1.99	😊 😊 😊
£2.00 to £2.99	😊 😊 😊 😊 (
£3.00 to £3.99	😊 😊 😊 😊 😊 (
£4.00 to £4.99	😊 (

Key: 😊 = 5 people

a) How many people get £1.00 to £1.99?

b) Estimate how many people get £2.00 to £2.99.

c) Estimate how many people get £4.00 to £4.99.

LINE GRAPHS AND PIE CHARTS

HANDLING DATA 3

1. The school secretary kept a record of the number of telephone calls she had to answer each day for ten days. She put the results on a line graph.

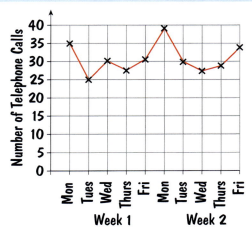

   a) On how many days did she receive thirty or more telephone calls?

   b) What is the greatest number of phone calls she received in one day?

   c) Which day of the week received the smallest number of calls?

2. Lee collected data on how many packets of crisps were sold each day for ten days in the school tuck shop. He recorded his data in a table. Draw a line graph for Lee's results.

Day	Number of Packets
Mon	35
Tues	27
Wed	28
Thurs	36
Fri	32
Mon	38
Tues	29
Wed	24
Thurs	27
Fri	30

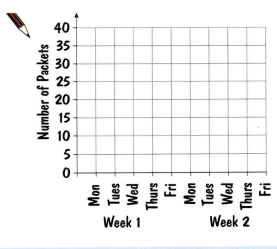

3. A newsagent works out how much money she gets from selling different items. She uses a pie chart to show this.

   a) Estimate what fraction of her income is from cards.

   b) If she gets a total of £800 a week, how much does she get from selling magazines?

   c) Estimate how much money she gets from selling sweets.

   d) Estimate how much money she gets from selling gifts.

Key Stage 2 reference: **Page 49**   Science Revision Guides - The Essentials of Maths Key Stage 2

TABLES

HANDLING DATA 4

1. Here is a table of items sold at the school office each day for a week.

	Monday	Tuesday	Wednesday	Thursday	Friday
Pens	9	3	2	4	6
Pencils	14	4	3	8	1
Rubbers	3	2	0	1	1
Rulers	5	1	4	3	2
Badges	8	22	5	11	4

a) How many rulers were sold on Thursday?

b) How many pens were sold in the week?

c) On which day were most items sold?

2. This table shows the distance in miles between six cities.

	Carlisle	Edinburgh	Exeter	Glasgow	Liverpool	London
Carlisle		98	346	97	125	307
Edinburgh	98		446	45	222	405
Exeter	346	446		444	250	170
Glasgow	97	45	444		220	402
Liverpool	125	222	250	220		210
London	307	405	170	402	210	

Use the table to find the distance from:

a) Glasgow to Edinburgh. _____ miles

b) Exeter to London. _____ miles

c) London to Carlisle. _____ miles

d) A salesman travels from London to Liverpool and then to Carlisle. How much further did he travel than if he had gone directly from London to Carlisle?

_____ miles

3. This table shows the times of buses from Kirkham to Blackpool.

Kirkham	0924	1124	1254	1554
Freckleton	0933	1133	1303	1603
Warton	0937	1137	1307	1607
Lytham	0946	1146	1316	1616
St. Annes	1000	1200	1330	1630
Blackpool Airport	1008	1208	1338	1638
Blackpool Bus Station	1028	1228	1358	1658

a) At what time does the 1254 bus from Kirkham arrive at St. Annes?

b) How long does it take to travel from Warton to Blackpool Airport?

c) I need to catch a bus from Lytham to get to Blackpool Bus Station before 1.00pm. At what time must I catch the bus from Lytham?

AVERAGES

HANDLING DATA 5

1. Kim has a job. She is asked to check that the mean (average) number of matches in a box is 48. She counts the number of matches in ten different boxes. This is what she found.

| 46 | 49 | 51 | 47 | 48 | 48 | 51 | 47 | 46 | 48 |

a) Calculate the mean number of matches. ☐ matches

b) What is the median number of matches? ☐ matches

c) What number of matches is the mode? ☐ matches

2. In a mental arithmetic test a class got these marks:

24 22 11 15 21 23 22 16 19 20 23 21 17 20 15
20 18 17 19 18 16 21 24 20 21 22 20 18 19 12

a) What is the range of these marks? ☐   c) What is the median test mark? ☐

b) Calculate the mean mark. ☐   d) Which test mark is the mode? ☐

3. Lucy is training for a swimming race. She swims ten lengths. These are her times for each length in seconds.

| 31.2 | 30.8 | 31.1 | 29.4 | 28.6 | 31.5 | 30.4 | 29.9 | 27.2 | 32.1 |

a) What is the range of these times? ☐ s

b) What is the median time? ☐ s

c) What is the mean time? ☐ s

4. Find five numbers that have a range of 5, a median of 16 and a mean of 15.

☐ ☐ ☐ ☐ ☐

5. The lowest night time temperatures in a Scottish Village over two weeks were recorded in this table.

| 2 | -3 | -5 | -1 | 0 | 2 | 4 | 3 | 1 | 0 | -1 | -2 | 2 | 5 |

a) What is the range of these temperatures? ☐

b) What is the mean temperature? ☐

PROBABILITY

HANDLING DATA 6

1. Here is a probability scale.

   Impossible |————————————↑————————————| Certain
                            A

   Show where you think each of these statements should be on the scale. The first one has been done for you.

   A "I am equally likely to get a head or tail when I toss the coin."
   B "I think I will probably pass my maths exam."
   C "It is unlikely to rain today."
   D "It could possibly snow tomorrow."
   E "There is quite a good chance of Michael winning his race."

2. Here is another probability scale.

   Impossible |————————————————————————| Certain

   Put these fractions and decimals on the probability scale.

   a) 0.5   b) $\frac{3}{4}$ c) 0   d) 1   e) 0.2   f) $\frac{3}{6}$

3. Estimate the probability of:

   a) The next dog you see being brown?
   b) The next cow you see being green?
   c) It raining in France in July?
   d) Winning the National Lottery?

   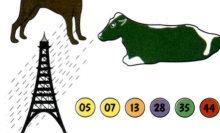

4. Stephanie estimated that the probability of the next bus being late is 1.8. Could she be right? Explain your answer.

FINDING PROBABILITIES

HANDLING DATA 7

1. A bag contains four red marbles, three green marbles and three blue marbles. One marble is taken out of the bag. What is the probability of getting:

   a) A blue marble?

   b) A red marble?

   c) A yellow marble?

2. A dice is thrown. What is the probability of getting:

   a) A score of 3?

   b) An even number?

   c) A number that is greater than 2?

3. Wilf has two spinners.

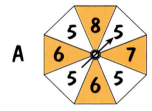 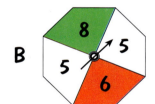

   a) What is the probability of spinning a 6 on spinner B?

   b) What is the probability of spinning a 7 on spinner A?

   c) On which spinner is he more likely to get an 8?

   d) On which spinner is he more likely to get a 5?

4. Wilma is designing a spinner. She wants the spinner to have the numbers 1, 2, 3 and 4 on it.

   She wants the probability of getting 1 to be $\frac{1}{2}$.

   She wants a 3 and a 4 to be equally likely.

   a) Put the numbers on the spinner for Wilma.

   b) What is the probability of getting a 2?

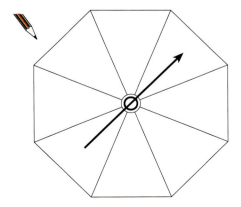

Key Stage 2 reference: Page 53   Science Revision Guides - The Essentials of Maths Key Stage 2   51

LISTING OUTCOMES

HANDLING DATA 8

1. Hannah has two spinners.

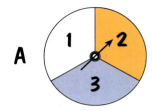
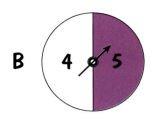

SPINNER	
A	B
1	4
1	5
2	4
2	5
3	4
3	5

The table shows all the possible outcomes. There are six possible outcomes. What is the probability of getting:

a) 2 on spinner A and 5 on spinner B?

b) A total score of 7?

c) A score of less than 7?

2. Simon's sock drawer contains two red socks and two blue socks. He pulls out one sock and then another sock without looking.

a) Fill in the table to show all the possible colours of socks.

First Sock	Second Sock

b) What is the probability of both socks being blue?

c) What is the probability of the socks being a different colour?

3. Maureen throws a dice and then spins this spinner. She adds the two scores together.

Here is a table to show all the possible totals. Use the table to answer these questions.

a) Is she more likely to get a total of 3 or 10?

		DICE					
		1	2	3	4	5	6
SPINNER	1	2	3	4	5	6	7
	2	3	4	5	6	7	8
	3	4	5	6	7	8	9
	4	5	6	7	8	9	10

b) What other total has the same probability as getting a total of 4?

c) What is the probability of getting a total of 5?

d) What is the probability of getting a total that is greater then 6?

EXPERIMENTAL PROBABILITY

HANDLING DATA 9

1. Louise had a bag with coloured counters in it. She pulled a counter out, made a note of its colour and put the counter back in the bag. She repeated this ten times. Here are her results:

Colour	Tally	Frequency
Red	|||||	5
Blue	|||	3
Green	||	2
Yellow		0

Use this table to estimate the probability of the colour of the next counter pulled out being:

a) Blue _____   b) Yellow _____

Louise repeated the experiment again until she had got 100 results. This is her table:

Colour	Tally	Frequency
Red	||||| ||||| ||||| ||||| ||||| ||||| |||||	35
Blue	||||| ||||| ||||| ||||| ||||| ||	27
Green	||||| ||||| ||||| |||||		21
Yellow	||||| ||||| ||||| ||	17

Use this table to estimate the probability of the next counter pulled out being:

c) Blue _____   d) Yellow _____

e) Which estimates do you think are the most reliable? _____

Explain your answer.

_____

2. Here are two methods for finding the probability of something happening:

Method A: Using equally likely outcomes.

Method B: Doing an experiment.

For each of these events say which method you would use to find the probability of them happening.

a) The next car to pass by having at least one passenger. _____

b) Scoring six when a dice is thrown. _____

c) A piece of toast landing "butter side up" when dropped. _____

d) The first two socks out of a drawer being a matching pair. _____

Following the recommendations of the National Numeracy and Literacy Strategies.

Pupil Worksheets to support "The Essentials of Maths - Key Stage Two."

Developed by a team of subject specialists with many years teaching experience.

Covering the pupils' needs at levels 3 - 5 Key Stage Two - and NOTHING more.

LONSDALE SCHOOL REVISION GUIDES

P.O. Box 7, Kirkby Lonsdale, Lancashire LA6 2GD
Tel: 015242 72230 Fax: 015242 72810
email: orders@lonsdalesrg.demon.co.uk

ISBN 1-903068-15-0

Published by Lonsdale Revision Guides

For other publications in this series see the inside front cover